If I Were a
Major League
Baseball Player

by Eric Braun   illustrated by Sharon Harmer

Special thanks to our adviser for his expertise:

Terry Flaherty, Ph.D., Professor of English
Minnesota State University, Mankato

Picture Window Books
Minneapolis, Minnesota

Editor: Shelly Lyons
Designer: Tracy Davies
Page Production: Melissa Kes
Art Director: Nathan Gassman
Editorial Director: Nick Healy
Creative Director: Joe Ewest
The illustrations in this book were created with traditional
drawing and digital painting.

Picture Window Books
151 Good Counsel Drive
P.O. Box 669
Mankato, MN 56002-0669
877-845-8392
www.capstonepub.com

All books published by Picture Window Books
are manufactured with paper containing at least
10 percent post-consumer waste.

Library of Congress Cataloging-in-Publication Data
Braun, Eric, 1971-
If I were a major league baseball player / by Eric Braun ;
illustrated by Sharon Harmer.
p. cm. — (Dream big!)
Includes index.
ISBN 978-1-4048-5536-6 (library binding)
ISBN 978-1-4048-5708-7 (paperback)
1. Baseball—Juvenile literature. 2. Baseball
players—Juvenile literature. I. Harmer, Sharon. II. Title.
GV867.5.B73 2009
796.357—dc22   2009003586

Printed in the United States of America in North Mankato, Minnesota.
092010
005924R

If I were a major league baseball player, thousands of fans would watch me play ball.

If I were a baseball player, I would work in a ballpark. I would love the soft grass and warm sunshine. People would come to the ballpark just to see me and my team.

If I were a baseball player, I would race across the grass. The batter's hit would fly like a rocket toward the wall. I would leap up and grab the ball.

You're out!

If a fielder catches a batted ball before it touches the ground, the batter is out. There's a lot of open space in the outfield where a ball can drop. The best outfielders can cover every inch of the outfield.

If I were a baseball player, I would field a smash hit. I would stretch and dive to scoop up the grounder.

Nice stop!

If I were a baseball player, I would step into the batter's box and waggle my bat. The pitcher would reach back. He would fire a blazing-fast pitch. In the blink of an eye, I would swing.

If I were a baseball player, I would crack a home run. I would know it was gone from the sound my bat made. The fans would cheer as the ball shot out of the ballpark.

If I were a baseball player,
I would steal second base.

Watch the pitcher,
Wait ... go!

I would slide into the base
ahead of the catcher's throw.

16

If I were a baseball player, I would throw a nasty curveball. I would wind up and let it go—zing!

Over the plate for strike three!

Major league pitchers can throw different kinds of pitches. A fastball is fast—some pitchers can throw 100 miles (160 kilometers) per hour! A curveball is slow and tricky! It bends on its path to the batter.

If I were a baseball player, I would visit many different cities. I would eat at restaurants and sleep in hotels. My teammates would be like a family.

If I were a baseball player, I would play a game for my job. Win or lose, I would have a ball!

How do you get to be a
Major League
Baseball Player

People who want to play baseball in the major leagues have to practice a lot! Batters swing at thousands of pitches. They work on hitting curveballs, fastballs, and other pitches. They also work on recognizing strikes and balls.

Pitchers have to throw lots of pitches. All players practice fielding grounders and fly balls. They work on running the bases. They learn how to make good decisions on the field, like when to run and when to hold up.

People who want to play baseball in the major leagues exercise a lot. They need to be healthy and strong. They play baseball on a high school team. Most of them play in college, too.

Glossary

balls—pitches that do not cross over home plate within the strike zone

bases—the four objects a runner must touch in order to score a point (called a run); the bases are first, second, third, and home plate

batter—the player who stands with a bat near home plate and tries to hit pitches

curve—short for curveball; a pitch that spins downward as it gets close to the batter

fans—people who are very interested in something (like baseball)

fielder—a player who stands in the field while the other team is batting; fielders try to catch a batted ball

grounder—a ball hit by a batter that rolls or bounces along the ground

home run—a ball hit by a batter that flies over the outfield fence; the batter gets to run around the bases and score a run

pitcher—the player who stands on the pitcher's mound and throws the ball to the batter

steal—when a base runner runs to the next base during a pitch

strikes—pitches that cross over home plate within the strike zone

To Learn More

More Books to Read

Hill, Mary. *Let's Go to a Baseball Game*. New York: Children's
    Press, 2004.
Jacobs, Greg. *The Everything Kids' Baseball Book*. Avon,
    Mass.: Adams Media, 2006.
Thomas, Keltie. *How Baseball Works*. Berkeley, Calif.:
    Maple Tree Press Inc., 2008.

Internet Sites

FactHound offers a safe, fun way to find Internet sites
related to this book. All of the sites on FactHound have been
researched by our staff.

Here's all you do:

Visit *www.facthound.com*

FactHound will fetch the best sites for you!

Index

Look for all of the books in the Dream Big! series:

If I Were a Ballerina
If I Were a Major League Baseball Player
If I Were an Astronaut
If I Were the President